YOUR ONE AND ONLY HEART

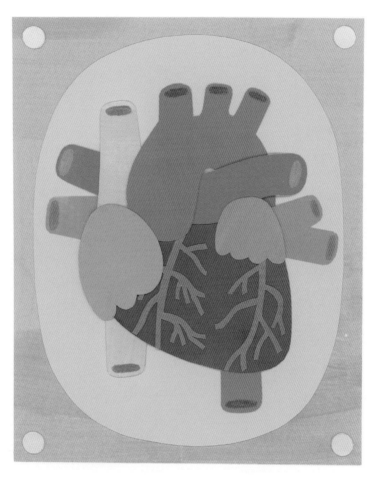

written by
Rajani LaRocca, MD

illustrated by
Lauren Paige Conrad

Dial **Books** for Young Readers

FOR LOU, JOE, AND MIRA: YOU ARE MY HEART — RL

FOR MY MOM, LIZ — LPC

Your heart is **SINGULAR.**

When you are born
and take your first breath,
your one and only heart is already beating.
It will beat every second
of every minute
of every hour
of every day
of your whole life.

Your heart is **COOPERATIVE.**

It's the captain of
Team Cardiovascular,
the system of tubes delivering blood
to every part of your body.
Your heart pumps blood
through thick-walled arteries
through capillaries, the tiniest tubes,
so oxygen and food
reach cells,
through floppy veins
that bring blood back
to be pumped out again.
The heart
is the heart
of this team.

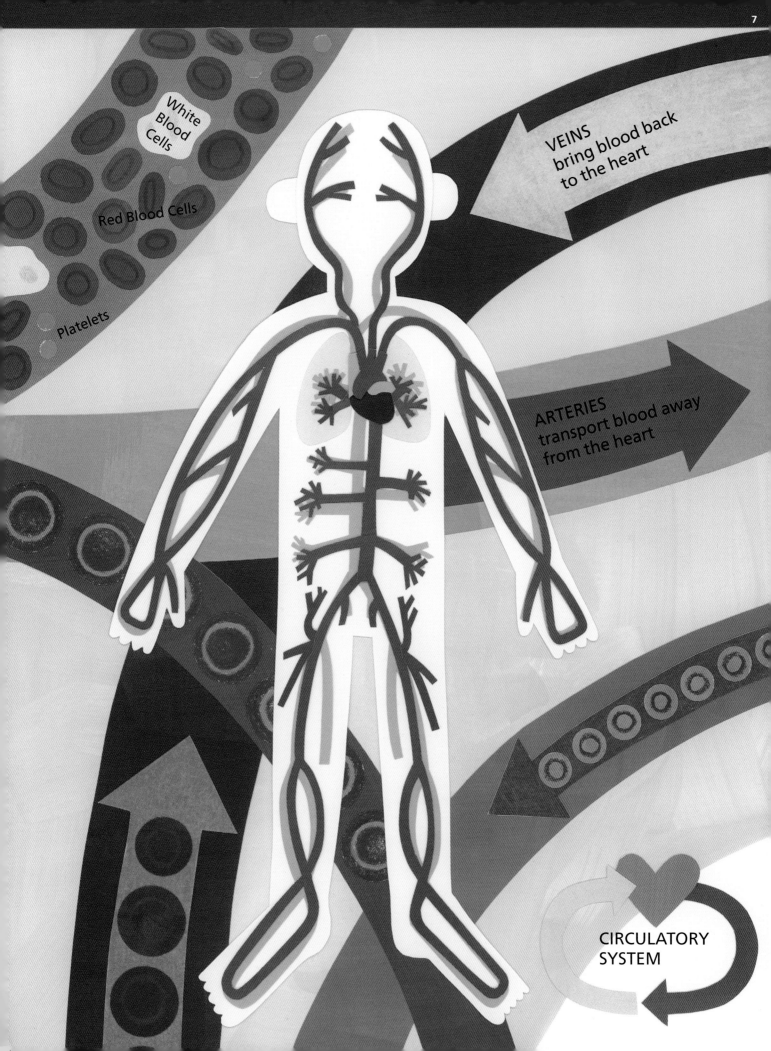

White Blood Cells

Red Blood Cells

Platelets

VEINS bring blood back to the heart

ARTERIES transport blood away from the heart

CIRCULATORY SYSTEM

Your heart is SIMPLE.

It squeezes, fills,
then repeats,
moving blood
to every part.
Your heart
squeezes, fills,
squeezes, fills,
repeats,
repeats,
repeats.

Your heart is COMPLEX.

It's the most remarkable pump
in the history of pumps.
Four heart chambers work in concert:
two on top, two on the bottom.
The smaller right side pumps to the lungs;
the larger left side, everywhere else.
Valves in between open, snap shut,
saying, "lub-DUB."

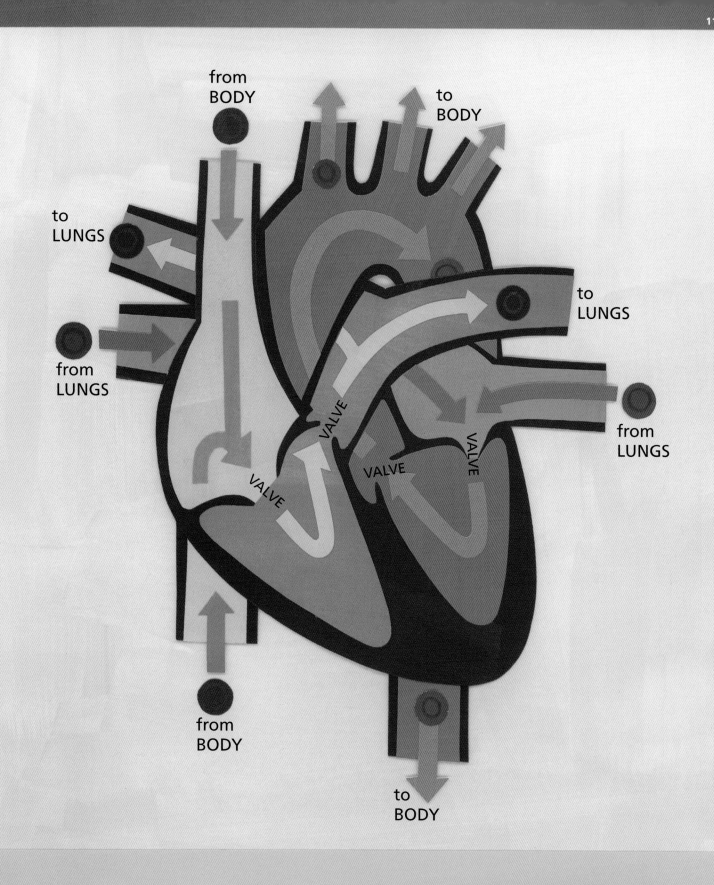

from
BODY

to
BODY

to
LUNGS

from
LUNGS

to
LUNGS

from
LUNGS

VALVE

VALVE

VALVE

VALVE

VALVE

from
BODY

to
BODY

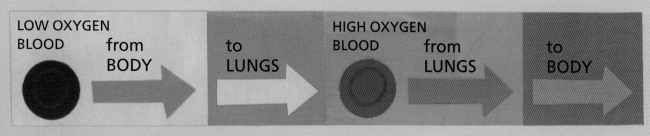

LOW OXYGEN
BLOOD   from
BODY   to
LUNGS   HIGH OXYGEN
BLOOD   from
LUNGS   to
BODY

Your heart is ENERGETIC.

It squeezes more than half its contents out
with every beat.
When it's excited,
it goes faster,
squeezes even more,
doing many times the work it does at rest.

Your heart is RELAXED.

Between each "DUB" and the next
"lub"
comes a crucial time
for the heart to relax,
to fill with blood,
so there's something to pump out.
Without relaxing,
squeezing doesn't work.
Consider a dropper:
If you don't fill it with liquid,
nothing can squirt out.

Your heart is **CONSTANT**.

Your one and only heart keeps
a constant pace,
consistent rhythm,
perfectly in sync.
So cells get blood
delivered right on time.
Slower paced for big bodies,
faster paced for small.

Elephant: 30 beats/min

Mouse: 310-840 beats/min

Child: 65-110 beats/min

Your heart is CHANGEABLE.

In response to
moving
sitting
thinking
playing
feeling
sleeping,
your heart speeds up
or slows down,
squeezes more
or less,
working like a hidden engine
or calmly beating
while you rest.

Your heart is ELECTRIC.

No need for a cord
or battery.
Inside your heart, chemicals move
to make electric signals
that spread in a coordinated way,
as if traveling on little wires,
to make your heart squeeze.
Top chambers first,
then the bottoms,
in the right order every time.

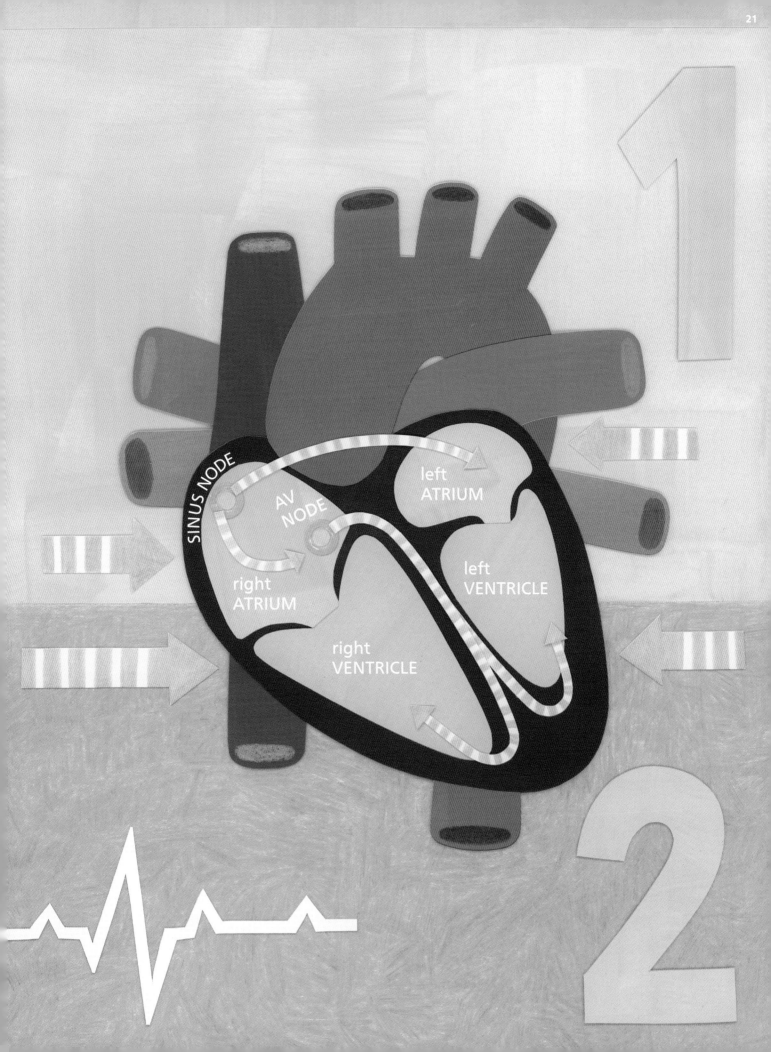

Your heart is MUSCULAR.

Tough,
built for endurance,
your heart is the hardest working,
most important muscle ever,
and it's the size of your fist.
Like other muscles,
to keep it strong,
you need to use it.

Your heart is HIDDEN.

Tucked in your chest
between pillowy lungs
in a protective cage of ribs.
Your heart is hidden because
it's so very
vital.

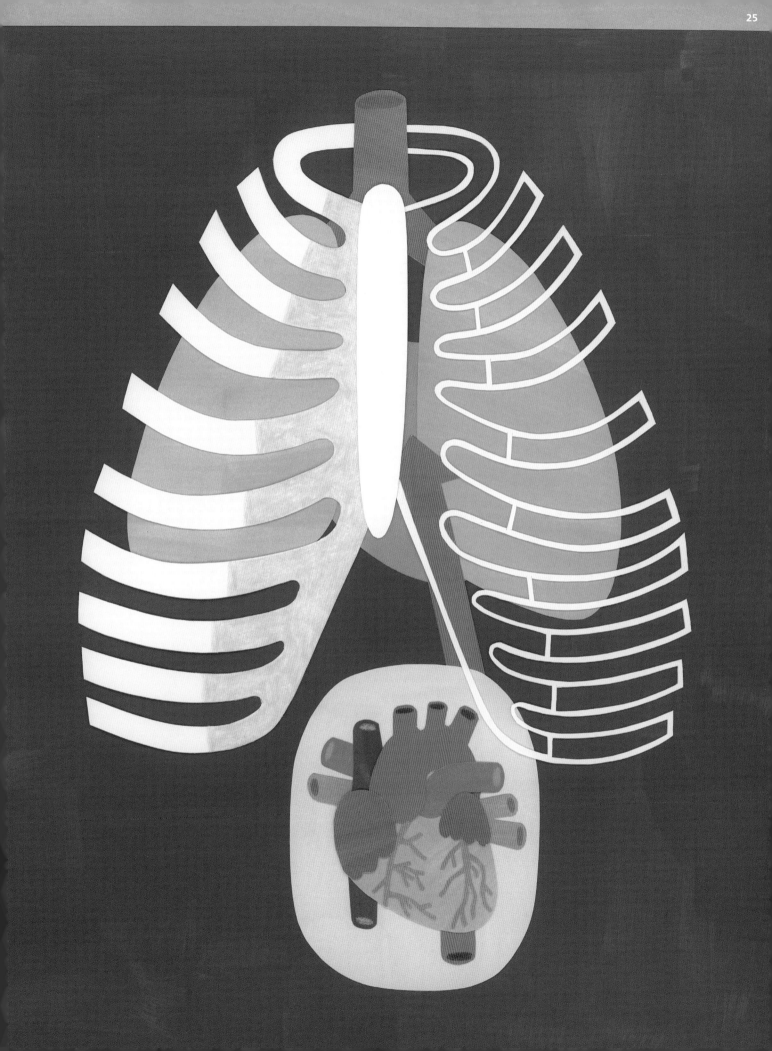

Your heart is NOTICEABLE.

You can see
and feel
and hear your heart at work,
if you know how to
look
touch
and listen.

Your heart is SELFISH.

The first offshoots from the largest artery,
before the big pipes that go
to the brain,
are tiny little tubes
that bring blood to
the heart.
After all,
the heart can't work
if it isn't fed
first.

Your heart is SELFLESS.

Oh, heart!
It toils away
while other organs
rest.
(Even the brain gets to sleep.)
But if the heart stops,
everything else does too.
So on it goes,
working away
every second
of every minute
of every hour
of every day
of your whole life.

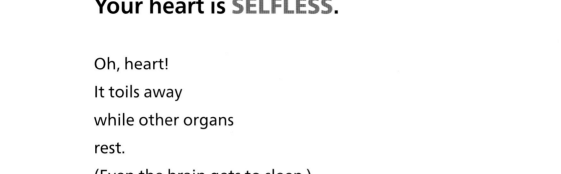

Your heart is
your one and only.
It is resilient,
enduring,
built perfectly for its important job.
And finally
after billions and billions and billions of beats,
when it stops at last,
so
does
life.

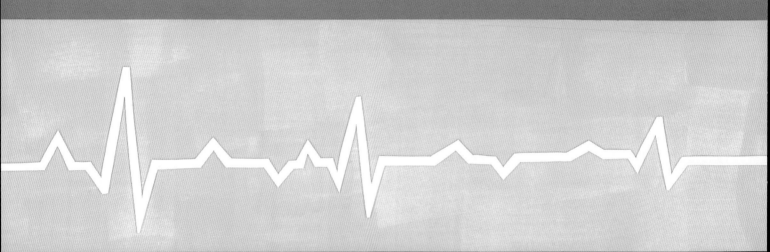

Your one and only heart is
SINGULAR and **COOPERATIVE**,
SIMPLE and **COMPLEX**,
ENERGETIC and RELAXED,
CONSTANT and CHANGEABLE,
ELECTRIC and **MUSCULAR**,
HIDDEN and **NOTICEABLE**,
SELFISH and **SELFLESS**.
And so, it does
Everything
it's supposed to do.

Just like you.

MORE HEART FACTS

COOPERATIVE

Your heart is part of a team called the cardiovascular system. *Cardio* means HEART and *vascular* means BLOOD VESSELS. Your heart pumps blood to the rest of your body through arteries—the biggest ones are the pulmonary artery (which brings blood to the lungs) and the aorta (which brings blood to the rest of the body). Arteries tend to be deep under your skin; you can't usually see them, but you can feel the push of blood through them, called a pulse. Arteries bring blood away from the heart.

Arteries branch into smaller arteries, and then even smaller blood vessels called arterioles, until they become the tiniest blood vessels in the body—capillaries, which are so small that gases like oxygen and carbon dioxide can pass through their walls, and glucose can be delivered to hungry cells.

Capillaries join to form larger blood vessels called venules, which join to form veins, which bring blood back to the heart to start the whole process over again! You can sometimes see smaller veins under the surface of your skin; they may look a little blue. The largest veins in the body are the superior vena cava and the inferior vena cava.

SINGULAR

The heart is the first organ to start functioning. It beats around 54 million times before you are even born. Over the course of your life, your heart will beat 3.2 billion times!

SIMPLE

Your heart is one of nature's most elegant and efficient pumps, delivering blood to every single part of you.

pg. 7

Circulatory System

SELFISH

The coronary arteries—the arteries that supply blood to the heart—are the very first branches off the aorta. When these arteries get clogged, a person can have a heart attack, or myocardial infarction, where part of the heart muscle dies. This is a serious condition, but doctors can treat it with medications and procedures to unclog the arteries.

SELFLESS

Although your heart slows down a lot at night while you're sleeping, it doesn't stop beating. Luckily, you never have to think about it! Your "pacemaker" and the autonomic nervous system keep it working even while you rest.

When a person's heart stops for more than two or three minutes, they die—because that's the limit of how long the brain can go without oxygen. The lack of a heartbeat or pulse is the main sign that someone has died.

OUTER HEART

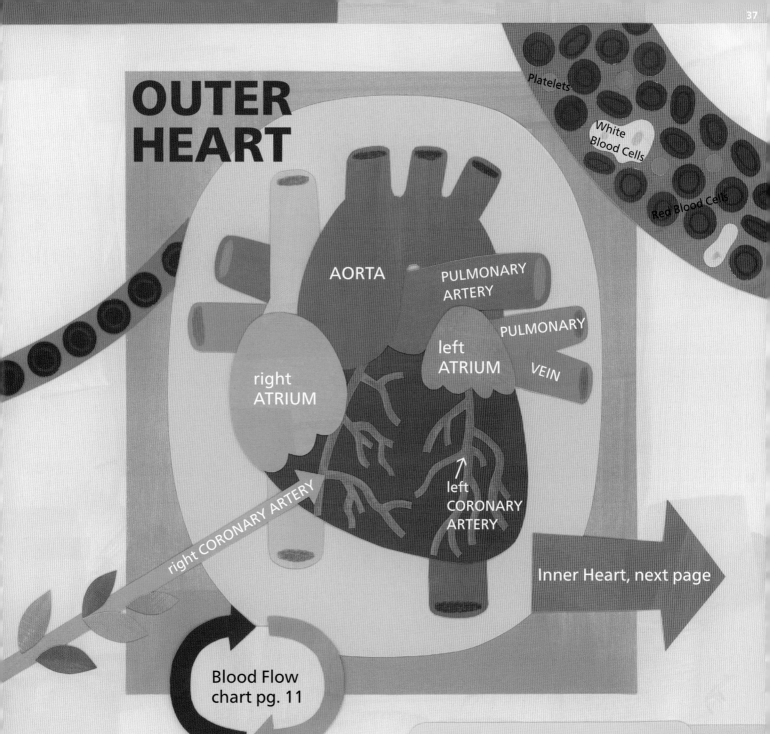

Platelets

White Blood Cells

Red Blood Cells

AORTA

PULMONARY ARTERY

PULMONARY VEIN

left ATRIUM

right ATRIUM

right CORONARY ARTERY

left CORONARY ARTERY

Inner Heart, next page

Blood Flow chart pg. 11

ENERGETIC

Your heart works to get blood where it needs to go: your muscles when you're running, your brain when you're thinking, and your intestines when you're digesting. When you exercise hard, your heart can pump four to six times as much as normal!

RELAXED

Relaxing is just as important as working! If the heart didn't fill up with blood between squeezes, it wouldn't have anything to squeeze. The time when the heart squeezes is called systole. The time between the squeezes, which is longer, is called diastole.

CHANGEABLE

Before you even move a muscle, your heart can change how it pumps in anticipation. Nerves from the autonomic nervous system go from your brain to your heart, so thoughts and emotions can affect how your heart is working. This is probably why people say strong emotions come from our hearts—because we can feel our heartbeats change in response to our emotions.

MUSCULAR

Using a muscle makes it stronger. You can help keep your heart in its best shape by exercising every day, so play! Regular exercise also helps keep your blood vessels, large and small, in great shape too.

CONSTANT

Your heart's regular rhythm allows it to fill, squeeze, and deliver blood efficiently. Smaller organisms tend to have faster heartbeats than bigger ones. Babies' hearts beat 100–160 times per minute; older children's hearts go at 65–110 beats per minute, and grownups are typically 55–90. A mouse's heart races at 310-840 beats per minute! And an elephant's? Just 30.

ELECTRIC

Your heart works through electricity! A special area in the top of the heart called the sinus node, the "pacemaker" of the heart, sets the heart rate. Electrical signals travel to the atria first, then the ventricles. These electrical signals travel to the rest of the heart muscle, which contracts because of more electric signals.

You can "see" the electrical signals in the heart with an electrocardiogram (EKG). An *arrythmia* is when something goes wrong with the heart's rhythm. Some arrythmias don't affect the heart's function; others can be life-threatening. If someone's sinus node is beating too slowly, an external pacemaker can be used to maintain a normal rhythm. When someone's heart is an a dangerous arrythmia called *ventricular fibrillation*, the heart is completely unable to work, and the person may die. People can perform *cardio-pulmonary resuscitation* (CPR) to keep blood flowing to the brain until the heart can be restarted. A *defibrillator* can deliver a jolt of electricity to reset the heart into a normal rhythm to get it beating again.

HIDDEN

The heart and brain are our most important organs, so our bodies evolved to keep them safe. The brain is encased in a hard skull, but the heart and lungs need to move, so they are protected in a rib cage that gives them room.

pg. 25—27

NOTICEABLE

You can sometimes SEE your heartbeat in your neck or wrist, especially if you've been exercising. You can FEEL your heartbeat by putting your hand on the left side of your chest. You can also feel your PULSE (the blood being pushed through arteries) in your neck, wrist, feet, and other places. You can HEAR your heart if you put your ear to someone's chest or use a stethoscope. You hear lub-DUB, lub-DUB, the sounds of the valves shutting when the heart squeezes and relaxes.

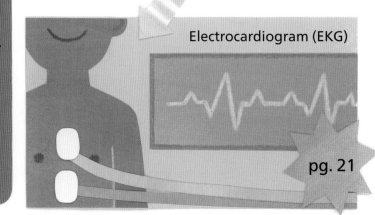

Electrocardiogram (EKG)

pg. 21

INNER HEART

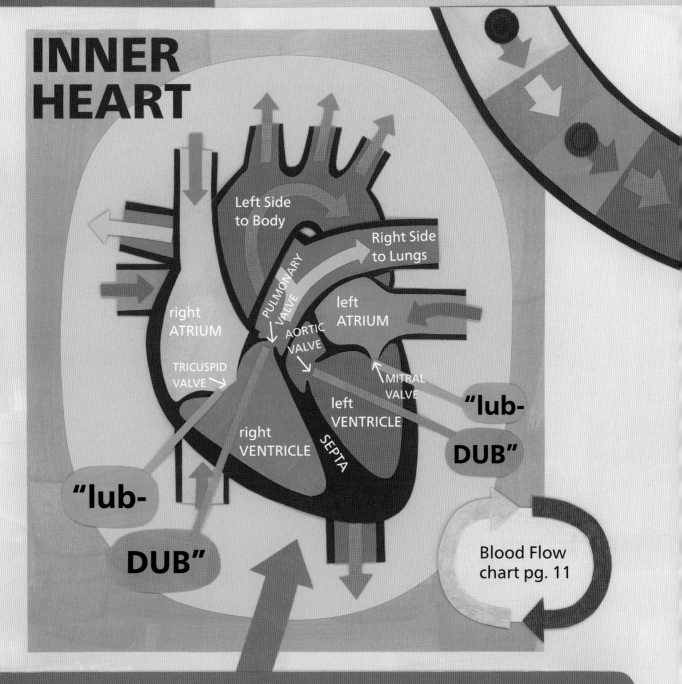

Left Side to Body

Right Side to Lungs

PULMONARY VALVE

right ATRIUM

left ATRIUM

AORTIC VALVE

TRICUSPID VALVE

MITRAL VALVE

left VENTRICLE

right VENTRICLE

SEPTA

"lub-DUB"

"lub-DUB"

Blood Flow chart pg. 11

COMPLEX

Your heart is made up of parts that work in complex coordination. It's divided into the right side, which pumps blood to the lungs to pick up oxygen and drop off carbon dioxide, and the left side, which pumps blood to the rest of the body.

The heart is also divided into smaller upper chambers, called *atria*—and large muscular, lower chambers, called *ventricles*. The atria are the staging areas, holding blood and squeezing it into the ventricles at the right time. When the atria squeeze, the ventricles relax, and when the ventricles squeeze, the atria relax.

There are walls called *septa* between the left and the right sides of the heart, and one-way doors called *valves* between the atria and the ventricles and between the ventricles and the big arteries. The valves shut when the different parts of the heart are squeezing so blood doesn't go backward. When you listen to your heart, the sound you hear is the valves snapping closed! When people have holes in the septa, or if valves are too tight or leaky, this can sometimes cause murmurs, which are extra and unusual heart sounds.

DIAL BOOKS FOR YOUNG READERS
An imprint of Penguin Random House LLC, New York

First published in the United States of America by Dial Books for Young Readers,
an imprint of Penguin Random House LLC, 2023

Text copyright © 2023 by Rajani LaRocca
Illustrations copyright © 2023 by Lauren Paige Conrad

Visit us online at penguinrandomhouse.com.

Library of Congress Cataloging-in-Publication Data is available.

Manufactured in China

TOPL

ISBN 9780593326336

10 9 8 7 6 5 4 3 2 1

Design by Cerise Steel
Text set in Tazugane Gothic

The art in this book was created using gouache, crayon, colored pencil, and collage.